ILLUMINATIONS FROM THE BHAGAVAD-GITA

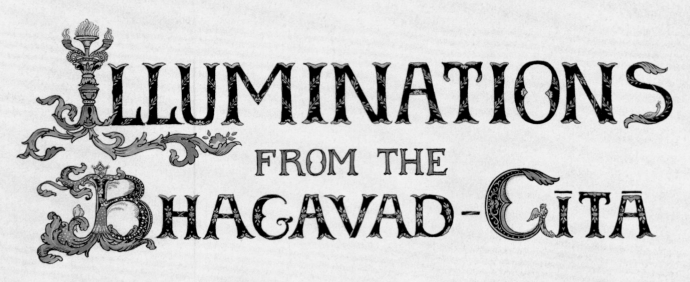

ILLUMINATIONS
FROM THE
BHAGAVAD-GĪTA

By Kim & Chris Murray

MANDALA
publishing group

San Francisco   Eugene   Singapore   Mumbai

Mandala Publishing Group
103 Thomason Lane
Eugene, OR 97404
phone: 800 688 2218
fax: 541 461 3478
mandala@mandala.org
www.mandala.org

1585-A Folsom Street
San Francisco, CA 94103
phone: 415 626 1080
fax: 415 626 1510

239C Joo Chiat Road
Singapore 427496
phone: 65 342 3117
fax: 65 342 3115

Grateful acknowledgment is made to the Bhaktivedanta Book Trust for permission to reprint excerpts from Bhagavad-Gita As It Is by His Divine Grace A.C. Bhaktivedanta Swami Prabhupada, copyright 1972 by Bhaktivedanta Book Trust.

ISBN 1-886069-21-2

Printed in China through Palace Press International

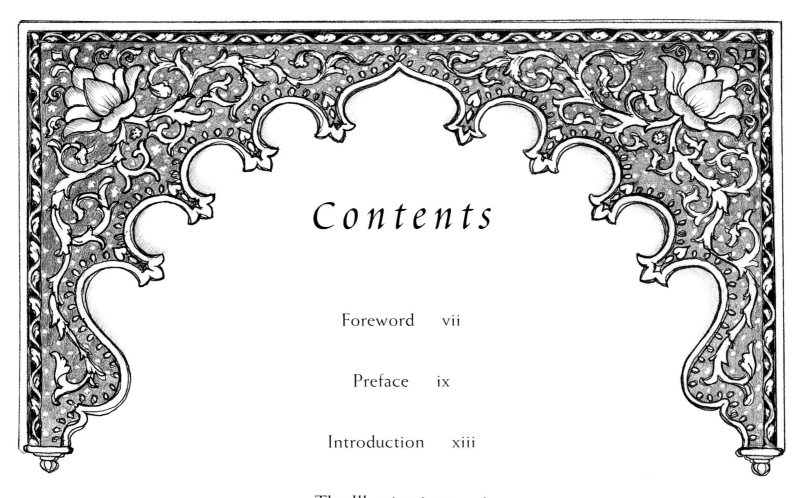

Contents

Foreword

eep within the forest comes the sweet sound of a flute. Like a tiny bird alighting on the smallest branch, the gentle music weaves a melody. And I am healed of care and woe. And I am soothed from constant thoughts of "me" and "mine". What is this sound? The "I" that "thinks" is mesmerized into a pleasant calm. My footsteps lead me where no path has been. Peacocks calling in the canopy. All creation bows to this sweet sound. Time stands still. The forest sighs. There within the deepest glade the blue child stands. Govinda! Garlanded, jeweled with crystal flowers. How His eyes they gaze upon all form. How His transcendental being glows, like a halo for the world to see. In Him I am free.

I write a spontaneous poem as I look at this wonderful work, *Illuminations From the Bhagavad-Gita*, by Kim and Chris Murray. How apt the title. To "illuminate" the wisdom from ancient Vedic literature. An inspiration for humanity today. Chris has selected the classic verses and brought his extensive knowledge of Indian art to this beautiful book. Kim, with her deeply emotional painting, has brought forth an exquisite vision of the Deity at play in our midst. We are enriched!

–Donovan 1998

Preface

Bhagavad-gita is like the sun, shining for everyone. It is not a sectarian doctrine, meant for a particular faith or class of people. It is the Song of God, meant for the enlightenment of us all. Bhagavad-gita is the essence of all Vedic literature. "Veda" means knowledge, and Lord Krishna, the original knower of the Vedas, is the author of Bhagavad-gita. By studying this transcendental literature we are learning from Krishna himself. Krishna declares in the Gita that "he who studies this sacred conversation worships Me by his intelligence."

Though first spoken long ago, Bhagavad-gita remains utterly vital today. It is not sentimental but is practical – a handbook of wisdom for our troubled times. Arjuna was experiencing many difficulties on the Battlefield of Kurukshetra. Today, we are likewise burdened with many serious problems. War, poverty, pollution and greed are everywhere, and getting worse. This is an age of anxiety. But the heart of the Lord is mercy and, in Bhagavad-gita, Krishna gives us the knowledge by which our activities may be purified and our suffering mitigated. If a person is interested in increasing his own happiness and that of society at large, the Gita can show the way. Krishna spoke Bhagavad-gita to take us from the darkness of ignorance to the light of knowledge—to illuminate us.

This book is a celebration of the glory of Bhagavad-gita and its author, Lord Krishna. Presented is a selection of verses from the Gita (which one should read in its entirety to fully relish its sublime philosophy) and a series of illustrations depicting some of Krishna's wonderful pastimes and activities.

Krishna's nature is transcendent. He is the Supreme Beauty who resides in everyone's heart. His form is all attractive and unlimited. In the spiritual world, love rules supreme. It is by love and devotion that Krishna may be known. This is the natural function of the soul. In such spirit, this book is offered to Krishna and to his intimate devotee, His Divine Grace A.C. Bhaktivedanta Swami Prabhupada, and his followers. If this book gives them some transcendental pleasure, then our efforts are a success.

–Kim and Chris Murray

Introduction

he time is five thousand years ago. The scene is a battlefield at Kurukshetra, India. A chariot bearing charioteer and archer sits between the opposing phalanxes of two mighty armies.

The battle which is about to begin is the inevitable climax of years of political intrigue. It is a fratricidal war to determine who will occupy the throne: righteous Yudhisthira, who is the eldest son of the dead King Pandu and the rightful heir, or his treacherous cousin, Duryodhana, who is trying to usurp the kingdom. Conchshells, bugles, and drums sound as two huge military forces poise for battle. From his chariot between the armies, the archer, Arjuna, beholds the soldiers on the enemy's side — many of whom are his own relatives — and he becomes overwhelmed with compassion and familial affection. Weeping, he lays down his weapons and refuses to fight.

At this point *Bhagavad-gita* begins. Arjuna humbles himself before his chariot driver, who we learn is no ordinary charioteer but the Supreme Personality of Godhead Himself, Lord Krishna. Accepting Lord Krishna as his spiritual master, Arjuna asks for help in his moment of crisis, and for one hour the world stands still as the Lord instructs Arjuna, and subsequently all mankind, in the wisdom of *Bhagavad-gita*, the Song of God.

> *The Supreme Lord said: While speaking learned words, you are mourning for what is not worthy of grief. Those who are wise lament neither for the living nor the dead. Never was there a time when I did not exist, nor you, nor all these kings; nor in the future shall any of us cease to be.*

Thus a momentous dialogue ensues as Lord Krishna explains the science of the spiritual soul, the material nature, and the Supreme Personality of Godhead, who controls both the spiritual and the material. Lord Krishna says: "I shall now declare to you in full this knowledge both phenomenal and noumenal, by knowing which there shall remain nothing further to be known."

Today, fifty centuries later, *Bhagavad-gita* remains the world's most complete book of scientific spiritual knowledge. Within India's great treasure house of human understanding, the Vedic literature, *Bhagavad-gita* is perennially the most popular book. In the West, the *Gita* has had profound influence on philosophy and literature and has been studied by virtually all of our major thinkers for the past two hundred years.

The present volume, *Illuminations From the Bhagavad-gita*, is appropriately titled, since the *Gita's* teachings are indeed illuminating. As one verse says: "When one is enlightened with the knowledge by which nescience is destroyed, then his knowledge reveals everything, as the sun lights up everything in the daytime."

That these verse translations are taken from *Bhagavad-gita As It Is* by His Divine Grace A.C. Bhaktivedanta Swami Prabhupada, makes the book doubly illuminating. A shroud of mystical jargon, which is nothing more than imprecise, impersonal rhetoric, obscures most English translations of the *Gita*, but here the translations are refreshingly lucid – illuminating. The reader comes away enriched with the wisdom of *Bhagavad-gita*, not puzzled by riddles. These illuminations, designed and painted by Kim and Chris Murray, wed tastefully with each verse, as page after page radiates with the wisdom and beauty of *Bhagavad-gita*.

Far more than just a picture book, these rich pages illumine many of the *Gita's* eternal truths. Here are a few of them.

The soul is eternal:

> *For the soul there is never birth nor death. Nor, having once been, does he ever cease to be. He is unborn, eternal, ever-existing, undying and primeval. He is not slain when the body is slain.*

The soul is our permanent identity throughout this lifetime, and at death we transmigrate to another body:

> *As the embodied soul continually passes, in this body, from boyhood to youth to old age, the soul similarly passes into another body at death. The self-realized soul is not bewildered by such a change.*

Lord Krishna is the father of all souls, the source of creation, and the all-powerful controller:

Of all that is material and all that is spiritual in this world, know for certain that I am both its origin and dissolution.

I am the generating seed of all existences. There is no being — moving or unmoving — that can exist without Me.

Lord Krishna's immanence can be perceived throughout His creation:

Know that all beautiful, glorious, and mighty creations spring from but a spark of My splendor.

Lord Krishna, as the Supersoul, accompanies each transmigrating soul from one body to another:

The Supreme Lord is situated in everyone's heart, and is directing the wanderings of all living entities.

Lord Krishna enlightens His worshippers from within their hearts:

Out of compassion for them (the constantly devoted souls), I, dwelling within their hearts, destroy with the shining lamp of knowledge the darkness born of ignorance.

He also enlightens these devoted souls from without through His representative, the spiritual master:

Just try to learn the truth by approaching a spiritual master. Inquire from him submissively and render service unto him. The self-realized soul can impart knowledge unto you because he has seen the truth.

Lord Krishna, although immanent, is simultaneously situated transcendentally in the spiritual world of bliss and knowledge. And the transmigrating soul, after having been perfectly enlightened by Lord Krishna (the Supersoul), the spiritual master, and *Bhagavad-gita*, can also return to the spiritual world:

One who knows the transcendental nature of My appearance and activities does not, upon leaving the body, take his birth again in this material world, but attains My eternal abode.

—Satsvarupa dasa Goswami

You cannot see Me with your present eyes. Therefore I give you divine eyes, so that you can behold My mystic opulence.

Bhagavad-Gita 11-8

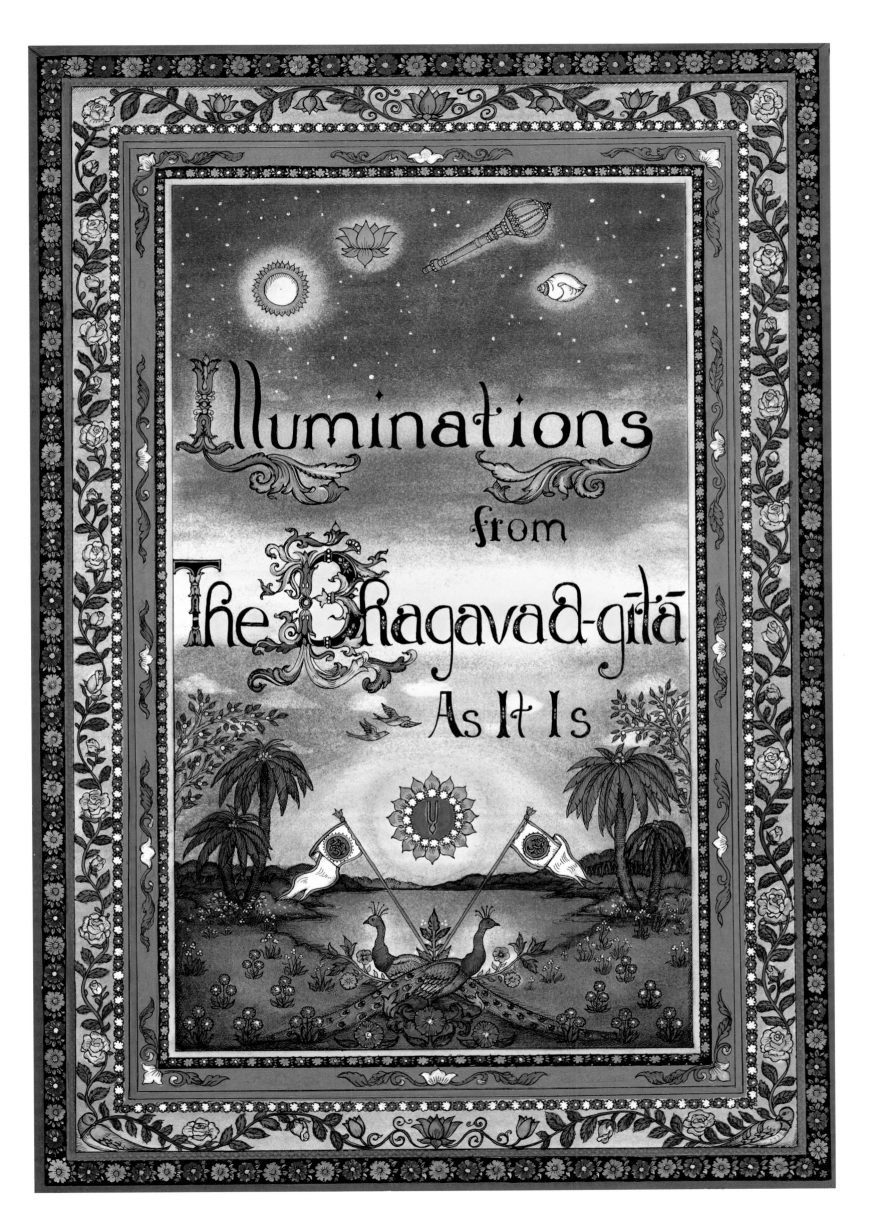

DEDICATION

TO

His Divine Grace

A.C. Bhaktivedanta Swami Prabhupāda

The greatest exponent of the
Bhagavad-gita and it's teachings
in the western world.

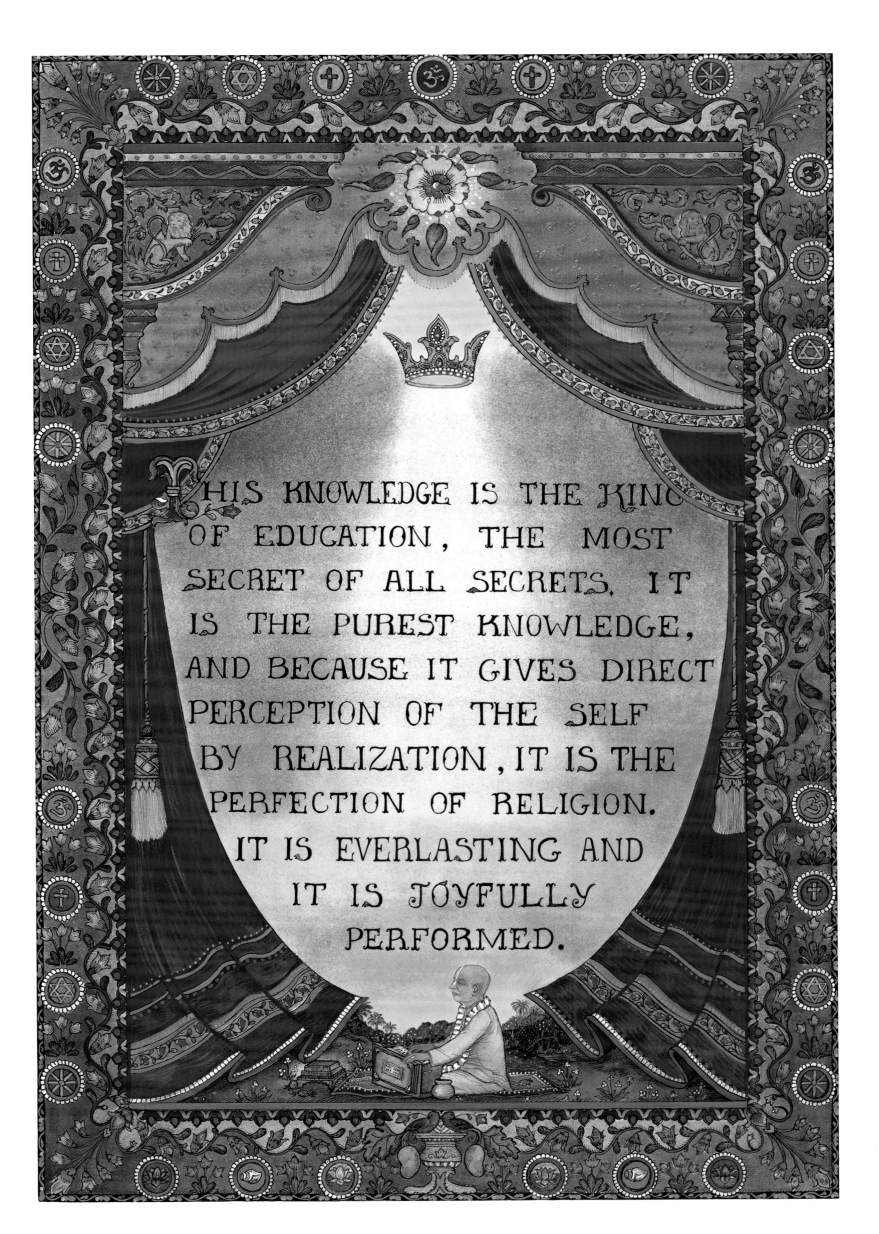

THIS KNOWLEDGE IS THE KING OF EDUCATION, THE MOST SECRET OF ALL SECRETS. IT IS THE PUREST KNOWLEDGE, AND BECAUSE IT GIVES DIRECT PERCEPTION OF THE SELF BY REALIZATION, IT IS THE PERFECTION OF RELIGION. IT IS EVERLASTING AND IT IS JOYFULLY PERFORMED.

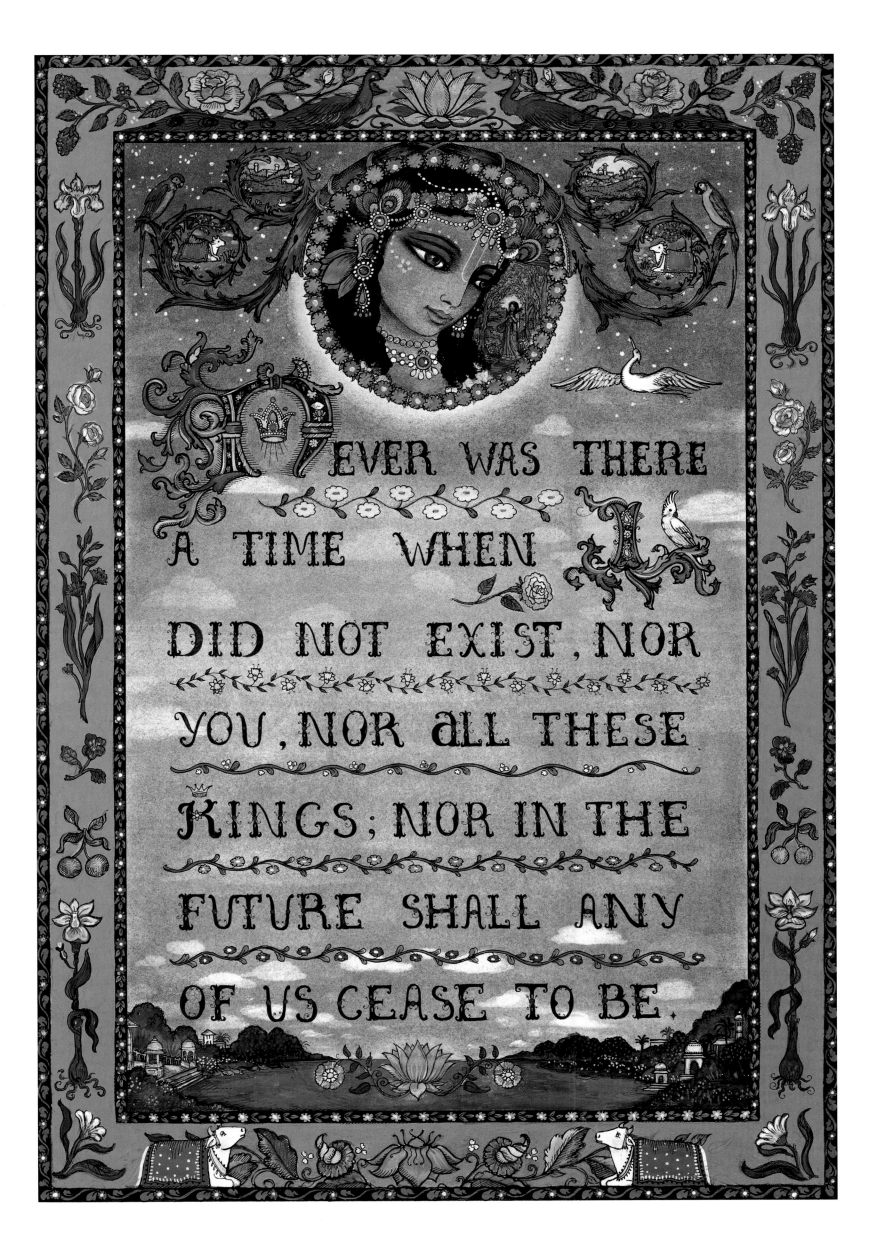

Never was there a time when did not exist, nor you, nor all these Kings; nor in the future shall any of us cease to be.

As the embodied soul
continually passes,
in this body,
from boyhood to youth
to old age,
the soul similarly passes
into another body
at death.

The self realized soul
is not bewildered
by such a change.

For the soul there is never birth nor death nor, having once been, does he ever cease to be. He is unborn, eternal, ever-existing, undying and primeval. He is not slain when the body is slain.

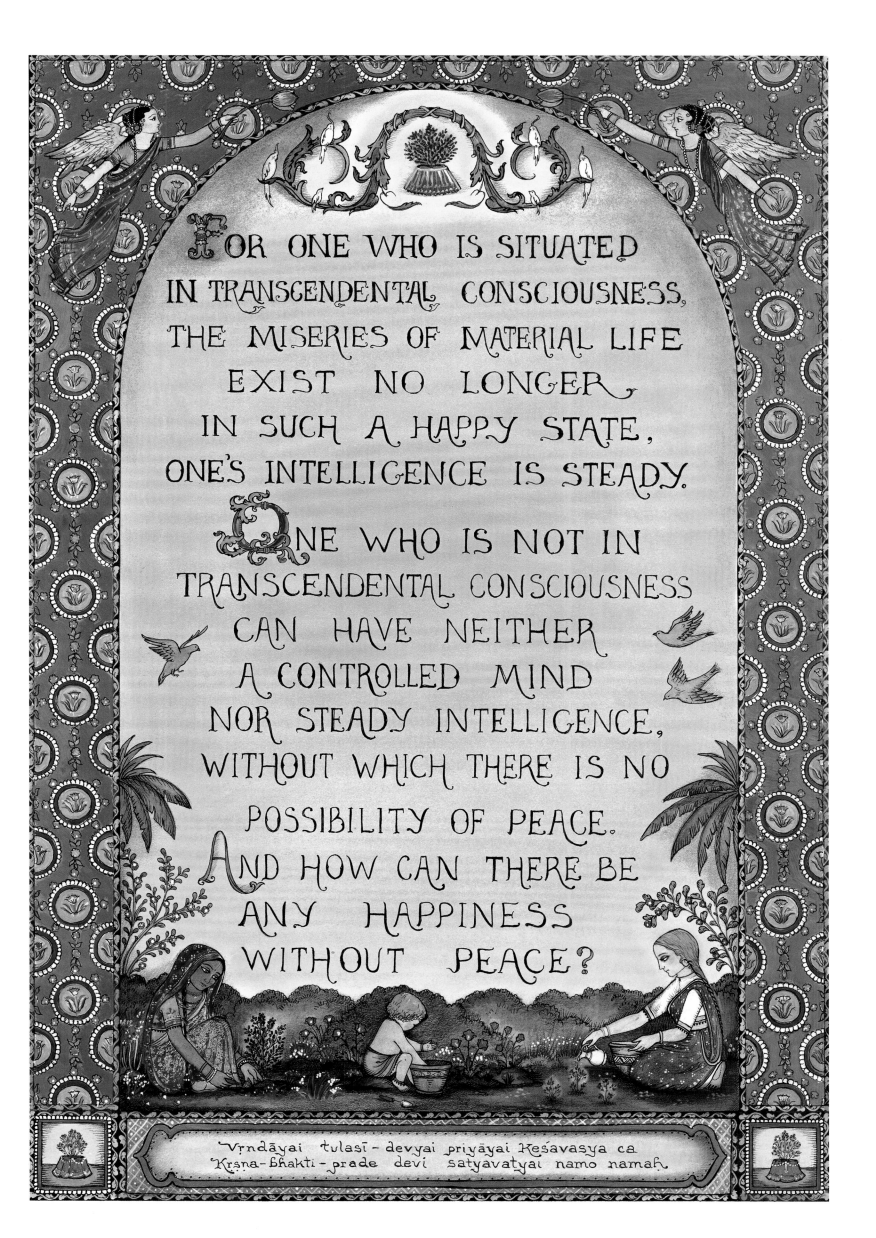

For one who is situated in transcendental consciousness, the miseries of material life exist no longer. In such a happy state, one's intelligence is steady.

One who is not in transcendental consciousness can have neither a controlled mind nor steady intelligence, without which there is no possibility of peace. And how can there be any happiness without peace?

Vṛndāyai tulasī-devyai priyāyai Keśavasya ca
Kṛṣṇa-bhakti-prade devi satyavatyai namo namaḥ

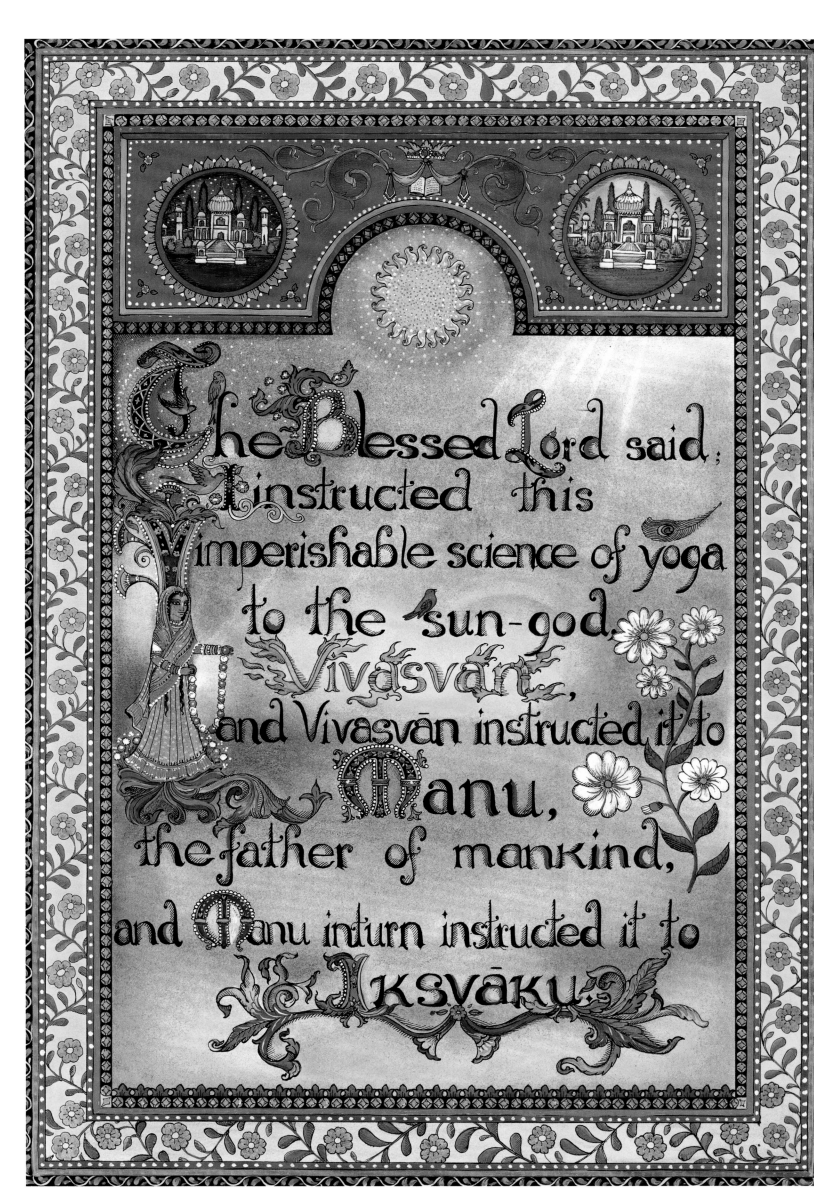

The Blessed Lord said; I instructed this imperishable science of yoga to the sun-god, Vivasvān, and Vivasvān instructed it to Manu, the father of mankind, and Manu in turn instructed it to Ikṣvāku.

That very ancient science
of the relationship
with the Supreme
is today told
by Me to you
because you are
My devotee
as well as my friend;
therefore you can
understand
the transcendental
mystery of this science.

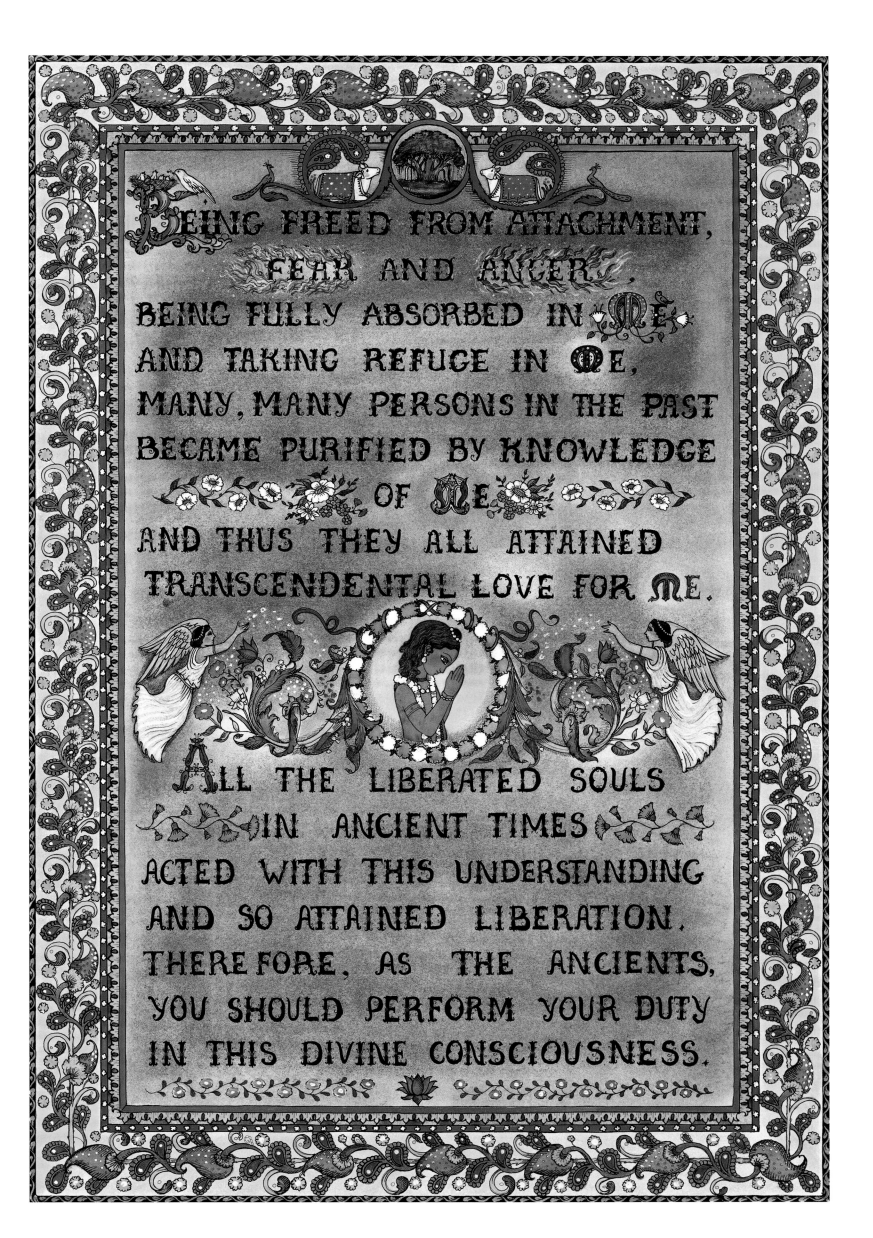

BEING FREED FROM ATTACHMENT, FEAR AND ANGER, BEING FULLY ABSORBED IN ME AND TAKING REFUGE IN ME, MANY, MANY PERSONS IN THE PAST BECAME PURIFIED BY KNOWLEDGE OF ME AND THUS THEY ALL ATTAINED TRANSCENDENTAL LOVE FOR ME.

ALL THE LIBERATED SOULS IN ANCIENT TIMES ACTED WITH THIS UNDERSTANDING AND SO ATTAINED LIBERATION. THEREFORE, AS THE ANCIENTS, YOU SHOULD PERFORM YOUR DUTY IN THIS DIVINE CONSCIOUSNESS.

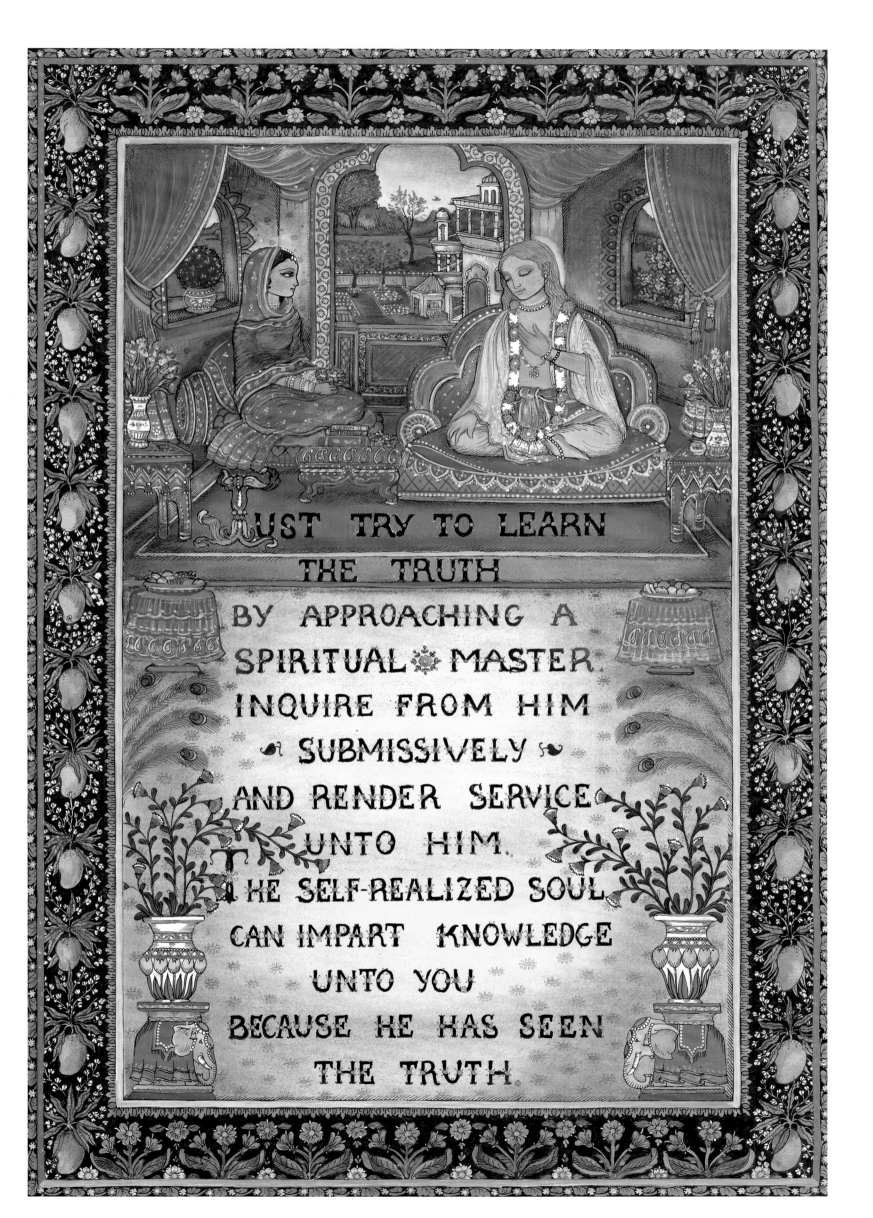

JUST TRY TO LEARN
THE TRUTH
BY APPROACHING A
SPIRITUAL MASTER.
INQUIRE FROM HIM
SUBMISSIVELY
AND RENDER SERVICE
UNTO HIM.
THE SELF-REALIZED SOUL
CAN IMPART KNOWLEDGE
UNTO YOU
BECAUSE HE HAS SEEN
THE TRUTH.

34

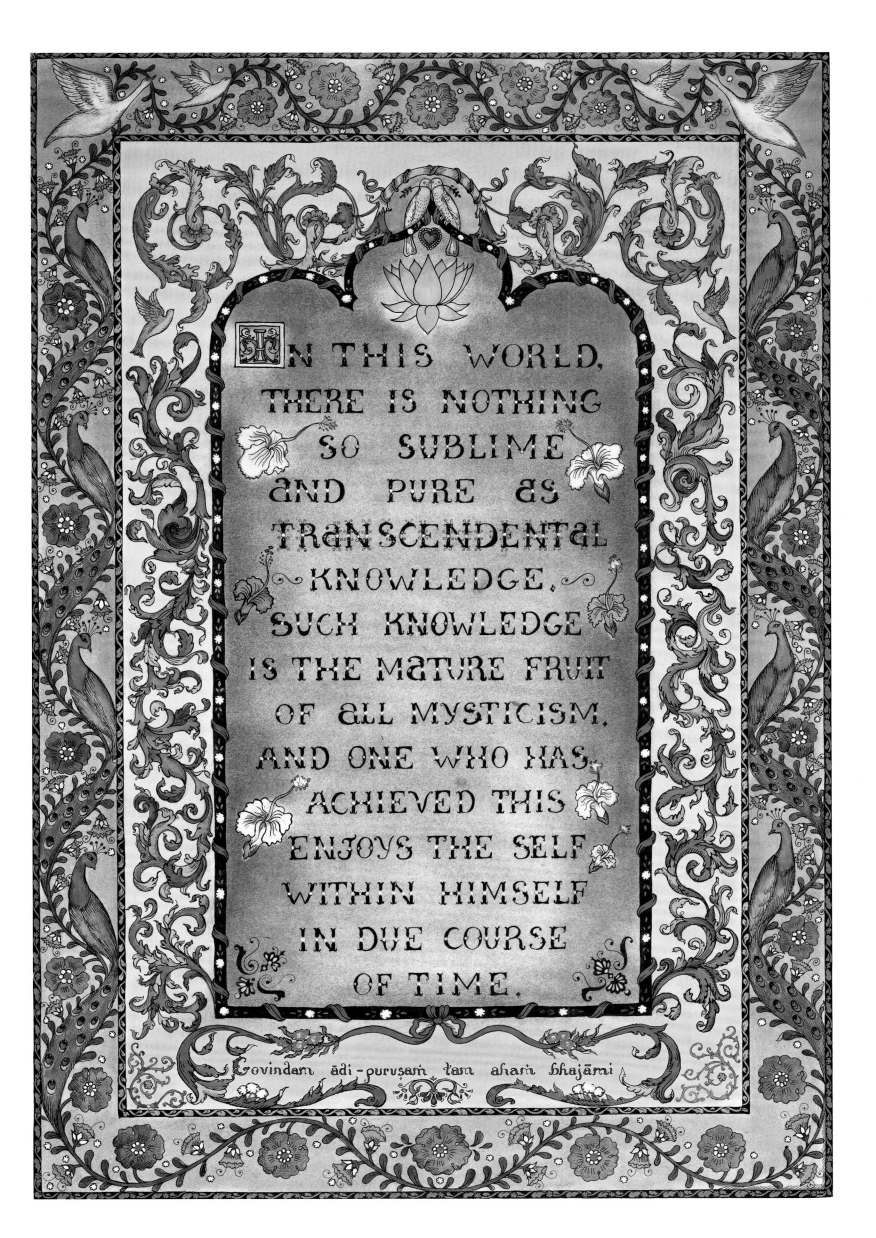

In this world, there is nothing so sublime and pure as transcendental knowledge. Such knowledge is the mature fruit of all mysticism. And one who has achieved this enjoys the self within himself in due course of time.

Govindam ādi-puruṣaṁ tam ahaṁ bhajāmi

One who works
in DEVOTION,
who is a pure soul,
and who controls
his mind and senses,
is dear to everyone,
and everyone is dear to him.

Though always working,
such a man
is never entangled.

When one is enlightened
with the knowledge
by which nescience is destroyed,
then his knowledge reveals
every thing,
as the sun lights up
every thing
in the day time

One whose happiness is within, who is active within, who rejoices within and is illumined within, is actually the perfect mystic. He is liberated in the Supreme, and ultimately he attains the Supreme.

A MAN MUST ELEVATE HIMSELF
BY HIS OWN MIND,
NOT DEGRADE HIMSELF,
THE MIND IS THE FRIEND
OF THE CONDITIONED SOUL,
AND HIS ENEMY AS WELL.

FOR ONE WHOSE MIND
IS UNBRIDLED,
SELF-REALIZATION IS
DIFFICULT WORK,
BUT HE WHOSE MIND IS
CONTROLLED AND WHO STRIVES
BY RIGHT MEANS
IS ASSURED OF SUCCESS,

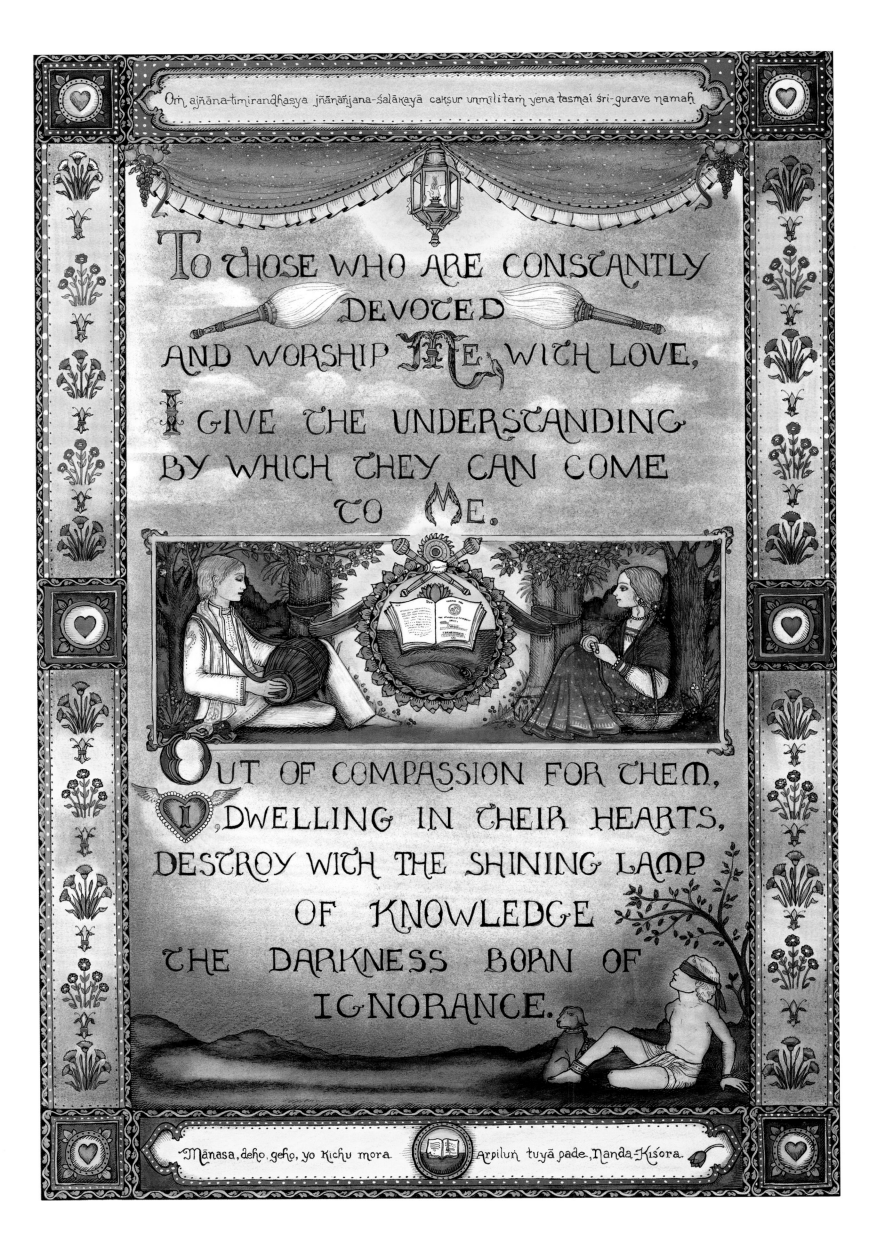

Oṁ ajñāna-timirandhasya jñānāñjana-śalākayā cakṣur unmīlitaṁ yena tasmai śrī-gurave namaḥ

TO THOSE WHO ARE CONSTANTLY
DEVOTED
AND WORSHIP ME WITH LOVE,
I GIVE THE UNDERSTANDING
BY WHICH THEY CAN COME
TO ME.

OUT OF COMPASSION FOR THEM,
I, DWELLING IN THEIR HEARTS,
DESTROY WITH THE SHINING LAMP
OF KNOWLEDGE
THE DARKNESS BORN OF
IGNORANCE.

Mānasa, deho, geho, yo kichu mora   Arpiluṅ tuyā pade, Nanda-Kiśora.

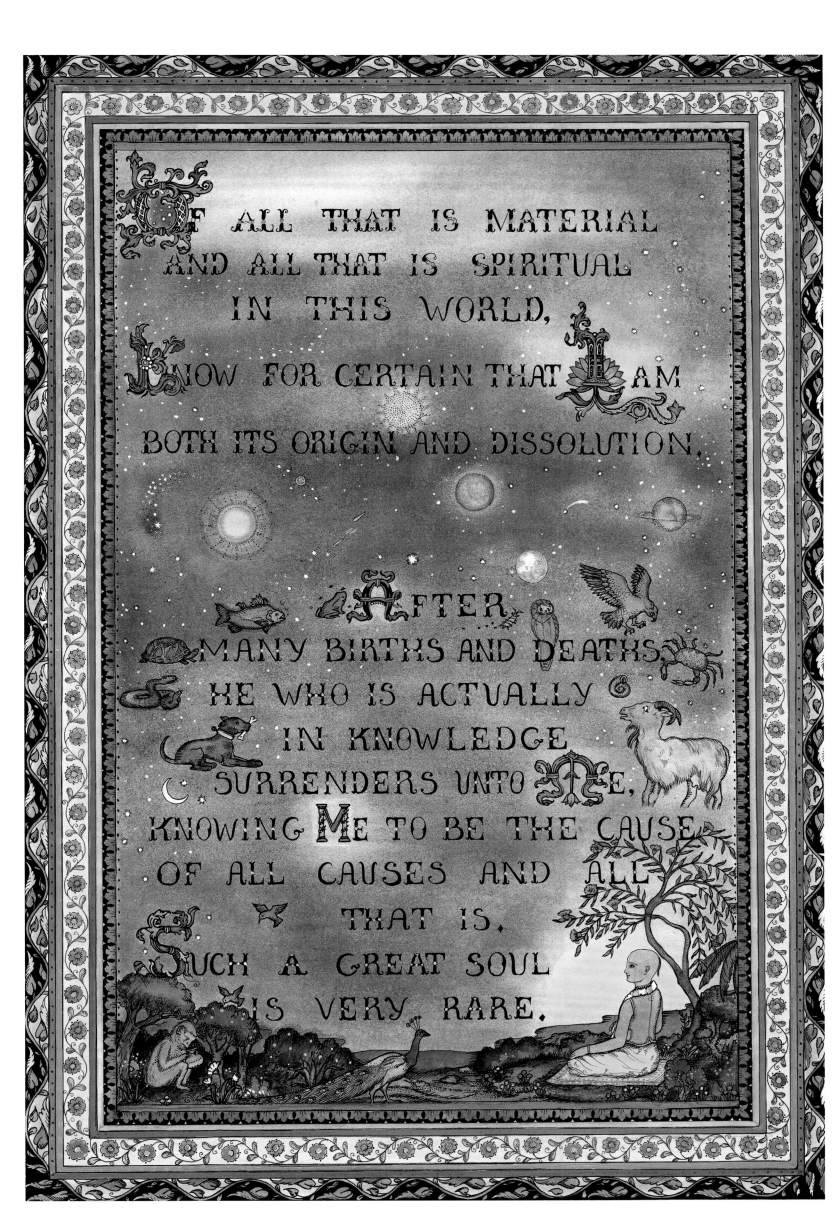

OF ALL THAT IS MATERIAL AND ALL THAT IS SPIRITUAL IN THIS WORLD, KNOW FOR CERTAIN THAT I AM BOTH ITS ORIGIN AND DISSOLUTION.

AFTER MANY BIRTHS AND DEATHS, HE WHO IS ACTUALLY IN KNOWLEDGE SURRENDERS UNTO ME, KNOWING ME TO BE THE CAUSE OF ALL CAUSES AND ALL THAT IS. SUCH A GREAT SOUL IS VERY RARE.

SHREEPAD SANATAN GOSWAMI PRABHUS BHAJAN KUTI

The thoughts of My pure devotees dwell in Me, their lives are surrendered to Me, and they derive great satisfaction and bliss enlightening one another and conversing about Me.

I am
the generating seed
of all existences.
There is no being
moving or unmoving
that can exist
without Me.

Know that all
beautiful, glorious, and
mighty creations spring
from but a spark of
My splendor.

The Supreme Lord is situated in everyone's heart, and is directing the wanderings of all living entities. Surrender unto Him utterly and by His grace you will attain transcendental peace and the Supreme and Eternal Abode.

Notes

About the Authors

Kim Waters Murray is a painter and sculptor who has been inspired by the artistic and spiritual traditions of India. Her work has also been influenced by Medieval and Renaissance paintings, as well as Pre-Raphaelite and Celtic art.

Chris Murray is the director of Govinda Gallery in Washington, DC, and has organized over one hundred exhibitions of paintings, drawings and photographs. His love for India and its spiritual culture has led him to travel there frequently.

Kim and Chris' personal association with A.C. Bhaktivedanta Swami Prabhupada, the renowned Acarya (Sanskrit for spiritual master), inspired them to create *Illuminations From the Bhagavad-Gita*. Swami Bhaktivedanta's translation of the *Bhagavad-Gita As It Is* is the basis for *Illuminations*. The authors first met Srila Prabhupada, as he is affectionately known, in London in 1971. They continued to study with Srila Prabhupada in India and in the United States until his passing in 1977.

Chris and Kim have collaborated on a children's book, *The Butter Thief*, also published by the Mandala Publishing Group.